Light the Sky, Firefly!

By Sheri Mabry Bestor

Illustrated by Jonny Lambert

T0028999

Pitter-patter,
drizzle-drip.

Summer rain cools the earth. Bees buzz. Birds glide.

*To Hailie, Kaiti, Whitnie, and Adam—who help
make each path on the journey more beautiful.*

—SMB

For Ezra—shine brightly.

—JL

Text Copyright © 2022 Sheri Mabry Bestor
Illustration Copyright © 2022 Jonny Lambert
Design Copyright © 2022 Sleeping Bear Press

Expert content review provided by Sara Lewis, professor of biology at Tufts University
and author of *Silent Sparks: The Wondrous World of Fireflies*.

All rights reserved. No part of this book may be reproduced in any manner
without the express written consent of the publisher, except in the case of brief
excerpts in critical reviews and articles. All inquiries should be addressed to:

SLEEPING BEAR PRESS™

2395 South Huron Parkway, Suite 200
Ann Arbor, MI 48104
www.sleepingbearpress.com

Printed and bound in the United States.

10 9 8 7 6 5 4 3 2 1

Library of Congress Cataloging-in-Publication Data on file

Names: Mabry, Sheri, author. | Lambert, Jonathan, illustrator.
Title: Light the sky, firefly / written by Sheri M. Bestor ; illustrated by Jonny Lambert.
Description: Ann Arbor, MI : Sleeping Bear Press, [2022] | Audience: Ages 4-8
| Summary: "Fireflies are some the world's most fascinating insects. And one many
children can find right in their backyards! With a simple story, perfect for read-alouds,
and colorful illustrations, this scientific look at a firefly's life cycle will captivate little
entomologists"—Provided by publisher.
Identifiers: LCCN 2021046791 | ISBN 9781534111158 (hardcover)
Subjects: LCSH: Fireflies—Juvenile literature. Classification: LCC QL596.L28 B47 2022
| DDC 595.76/44—dc23/eng/20211012
LC record available at https://lccn.loc.gov/2021046791

A firefly finds a place under the leaves that blanket the ground.

She begins to lay her eggs.

One, plop.
Two, drop.

Three.

Plop,

drop,

plop.

A female firefly can lay up to 500 eggs. She lays the eggs a few days after mating, in a moist environment such as wet soil under fallen leaves.

Under leaves, the eggs lay still.

For the baby fireflies inside the shells,
it is time to grow.

And begin to glow.

Fireflies produce a chemical reaction in their bodies called bioluminescence, which allows them to glow. Many species of fireflies are able to glow even before they are hatched.

Days end and begin again.
Weeks go by. Finally, the eggs hatch.

Out crawls one!

Then another!

And another!

Oh my! It's a baby firefly!

After about four weeks, in late summer, the eggs hatch.
The tiny insects that emerge are called larvae.

This firefly larva is hungry. He begins to hunt for food.

He finds a slug to eat. Squish.

He eats more. Squish.

The larvae hunt snails and slugs and other insects at night. Instead of fighting their prey, the larvae bite and then inject the prey with a liquid that keeps it from moving to get away.

And even more.

Squishy, squish, squish.

He grows.

As he grows longer, the days grow shorter.

Winter comes.

Snow covers the leaves.

But the firefly larvae stay safe, underground.

The larvae stay underground all winter—some make burrows in the dirt. They go into hibernation mode, which means they conserve energy to survive through the winter months.

In the ground, under the snow, the larva is still growing.

He sheds his casing.

He grows more.
And sheds it again.

Shedding an outer shell, or
exoskeleton, is called molting.

Finally, spring comes. Seeds sprout. Flowers bloom.

The baby firefly is ready to make his final change.

But first, he builds a nest.

He settles inside.

The larvae make a mud chamber, usually in late spring, when they are ready to pupate. The amazing transformation of changing from a larva to an adult firefly takes place. The beginning of this process is called histolysis.

On the outside of the nest, everything seems the same. But on the inside, everything isn't the same at all. . . . He is transforming!

When he is ready. . .

out he comes.

Oh my! It's a firefly!

Did you know that fireflies aren't flies at all? They are a type of beetle!

During the light of the day,
fireflies keep low to the ground.

When the sun begins to set,
they begin to climb higher.

Fireflies climb tall grass to launch from. They have hard forewings. They use them to stay balanced when flying.

And when the sky turns black, fireflies launch!

They use their strong wings to fly into the inky sky.

Fly high, firefly!

Most fireflies are nocturnal, so they are most active during the night, when it is dark. That is when you can see them lighting up the sky.

Uh oh!

A bird tries to eat this firefly!

But the firefly squirts out a white liquid.

Ick!

Nice try, but not this firefly!

When a firefly is attacked by a predator, a process can be set off called "reflex bleeding." Drops of white blood are shed from the firefly. These drops taste bitter to a predator. The fluid is also poisonous to some lizards and birds.

During their time in the sky, the fireflies light up.

Blink.

Blink.

Twinkle

blink blink.

They blink with their own rhythm, like a silent song.

Fireflies blink with specific rhythms called "flash patterns," and each species has its own. This helps them communicate with each other.

The sky is filled with flashing fireflies.

They twinkle like faraway stars.

Light the sky, firefly!

Some scientists use the chemical produced by fireflies for testing and detecting energy problems in human cells. This chemical is being used to study cancer, heart disease, multiple sclerosis, muscular dystrophy, and other diseases.

The twinkling and blinking tell some fireflies to stay away.

Blink.

Blink.

Twinkle blink blink.

Fireflies use blinking patterns to warn predators away, to defend their territory, and to attract a mate.

The twinkling and blinking tell some fireflies to come close.

Blink.

Blink.

Twinkle
blink blink.

This twinkling and blinking firefly attracts a female.

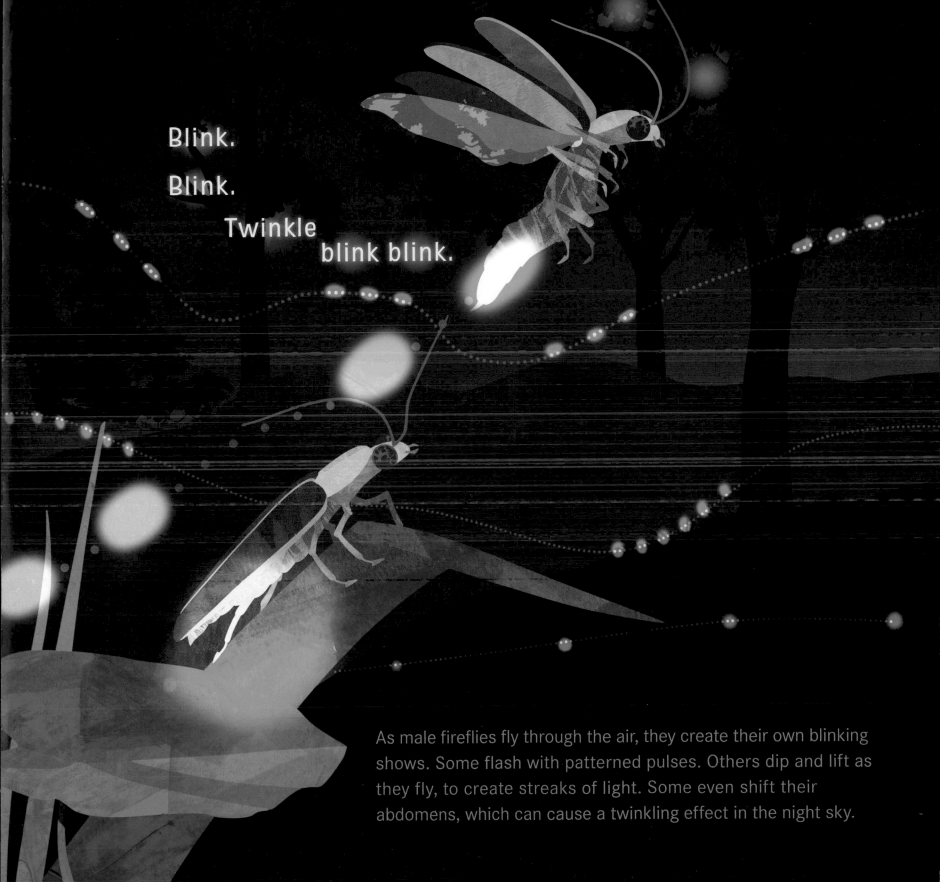

Blink.
Blink.
Twinkle
blink blink.

As male fireflies fly through the air, they create their own blinking shows. Some flash with patterned pulses. Others dip and lift as they fly, to create streaks of light. Some even shift their abdomens, which can cause a twinkling effect in the night sky.

In time, the females are ready to lay their eggs.

Pitter-patter,
drizzle-drip.

Summer rain cools the earth. Bees buzz. Birds glide.

A firefly finds a place under the leaves that blanket the ground.

Under leaves, the eggs lay still.

Firefly light is one hundred percent natural and, unlike the sun or other types of light, doesn't produce heat. Fireflies are the most efficient light source in the world!

For the baby fireflies inside the shells, it is time to grow.

And begin to glow.

For the adult fireflies...

The best way to enjoy fireflies is to sit very still during the evening and watch the blinking as fireflies light the night. While you may be tempted to try to catch them in a jar, letting them remain free keeps them safe, allows them to do what they need to do, and gives you a chance to appreciate the environment in its most natural state.

. . . it is time to go.

Bye, bye, firefly!